UNCOMMON PRAYERS

' An anthology of distinction.'

Public Opinion

' An anthology of unusual and delightful supplications.'

HOWARD SPRING, *Sunday Graphic*

' A careful collection of amazingly beautiful, simple prayers, taken from the past and present and from all the world.   This book is a treasure.'

John O' London's Weekly

UNCOMMON PRAYERS

Collected by

CECIL HUNT

LONDON

HODDER AND STOUGHTON LIMITED

First published March 1948
Eighth impression 1961

PRINTED AND BOUND IN GREAT BRITAIN FOR HODDER AND STOUGHTON, LIMITED,
BY RICHARD CLAY AND COMPANY, LTD., BUNGAY, SUFFOLK

AUTHOR'S PREFACE

THIS modest book has been in my mind, indeed on my mind, for several years. I hope that it may be a help and a pleasure to many on the by-paths that lead to the Damascus Road.

I am conscious that I have no qualifications for compiling this book beyond a love of literature and a belief that man is a trinity of body, mind and spirit, and that the godhead of this trinity is the spirit. Therefore I sought to enlist others amply qualified. All agreed that a book of uncommon prayers would be valuable, that there was no volume bringing together many of the much-loved pearls of prayer upon a common thread. But none, for differing and no doubt valid reasons, would approach the task. I have therefore done it myself, conscious of my inadequacy, conscious of the many omissions, although many of these are deliberate. The incomparable collects of Cranmer and some of the best-loved hymns in the various collections of the churches are omitted. They are easy of pursuit.

Many readers of this book will no doubt refer me to equally loved favourites of their own. The inclusion of all was impossible, for I believed, and the publisher concurred, that this book, to serve best its purpose, should be of handy size and modest price. It may be possible, if this book is acceptable, to include other equally cherished uncommon prayers in a subsequent volume. .

If I had been successful in securing the hoped-for compiler of this book, it would doubtless have been prefaced by a valuable and illuminating comment upon the jewel of prayer as manifested in the many facets here displayed. It would be presumption in me to attempt such instruction. The literature of prayer is an inexhaustible library, and it is available to all.

I think often of the woman described by Rousseau in his *Confessions*. He tells of a wise bishop who, during a visit to his diocese, came upon an old woman who, by way of prayer, could say nothing but " Oh ! " " Good mother," said the bishop, " continue to pray in this manner ; your prayer is better than ours."

Most of the uncommon prayers included here will be common to some ; not all, I trust, to everyone. There are pages left at the end of the book whereon further favourites and discoveries may be added. For such a book must, of necessity, assume a personal significance.

There are occasions that print a prayer indelibly upon the mind. I cannot repeat Queen Elizabeth's prayer without living anew the occasion when my friend, Clemence Dane, with her glorious voice and elocution, recited it in my parish church. It was a short Army leave that enabled me to visit my younger son at his half-term which prompted the discovery, in the magazine of St. John's and St. Mary's, Devizes, of the moving prayer written by the American soldier. I think of my friend, Commander L. C. Bernacchi, physicist to Captain Scott's first expedition, writing at my suggestion the *Saga of the " Discovery "*. He strove for many days to find a suitable line with which to preface this brave chronicle, and eventually decided upon the brief but eloquent French prayer to be found in these pages.

I think, whenever I hear the lovely " God be in my head ", of the packed Mother Church of England in October 1944, when thousands who loved him gathered for the funeral of William Temple, Lord Archbishop of Canterbury, Primate of All England.

The lashing rain, in which thousands had stood for hours, made the vast cathedral sombre and yet strangely luminous.

The lighted sanctuary shone like a dazzling jewel through the gates of the great choir screen.

As the coffin of the Archbishop was borne down the nave upon the broad shoulders of men of the Buffs, the choir sang this lovely prayer. The vast west doors moved slowly open. The rain revealed was so violent that the planned procession from the doors to Christchurch Gate was impossible, and the church dignitaries who were giving their last escort to a great leader, with Archbishop Lord Lang, were enveloped, isolated, lost in the slow surge of the vast sorrowing congregation. It was as though the sea of spirit had swallowed all that was material and personal, and the song of the tide was "God be at my end, And at my departing".

I was stationed at Canterbury at that time, and witnessed the wonder of thousands at the sparing of its glorious cathedral when so much destruction had laid waste its approaches and encroached almost to its doors.

I remember talking to the widow of a former canon who, on the morning after the City's ordeal of daylight dive-bombing, expressed to a Cathedral virger her thankfulness for the miracle of the Cathedral's preservation. " I knew it would not be harmed," the virger replied, " that day my wife and I saw angels on the Tower."

Some there have been, to whom I have related this incident, who have laughed heartily. So be it ; they are unlikely to read this book. We are still free to take our laughs where we wish to find them, but it would do none of us harm, perhaps, to include among our uncommon prayers the petition that we should never laugh at faith.

CECIL HUNT.

Salford,
  Chipping Norton,
    Oxon.

ACKNOWLEDGEMENTS

THE hymn " O God of Earth and Altar ", by G. K. Chesterton, is reprinted by permission of the Oxford University Press.

I am most grateful to Canon F. H. Gillingham, Rector of St. Stephen's Church, Walbrook, for permission to include the prayer " O God make the door of this house wide . . . " The author is unknown. Also to Miss Viola G. Garvin for her ready consent to the inclusion of her charming " Prayer for Michaelmas ". I thank Mme. Charles Jullien for the use of the " Bedouin Camel-driver's Prayer ", printed in her book *Once in Sinai*, which came to me in manuscript.

In an endeavour to supplement the acknowledgement already made to the author of the well-known " Refectory Grace " I uncovered some information that may be of interest. Chester Cathedral were unable to implement the recorded facts, but thought that the association with the Cathedral resulted only from Dean Bennett's discovery of the verses. This was endorsed by the Dean's son, the Rev. Frank Bennett, Rector of Wigan. He confirmed that the Dean, lighting upon the lines, and liking them, put a framed copy of the poem in the Cathedral. The verses were not used as a grace.

I do not think any copyright has been unwittingly infringed, but if it has it is not through lack of research, and any deficiencies will be gladly remedied in subsequent editions.

C. H.

UNCOMMON PRAYERS

The Lord is King : be the world never so unquiet.

MAKE clean thy thought and dress thy mixt desires !
Thou art Heaven's tasker ; and thy God requires
The purest of thy flour, as well as of thy fires.

Francis Quarles, 1592–1644.

LET all mortal flesh keep silent, and with fear and trembling
    stand ;
Ponder nothing earthly-minded, for with blessing in His
    hand,
Christ our God to earth descendeth, our full homage to
    command.

Liturgy of St. James.

All desire peace, but all do not attend to the things which bring true peace.—THOMAS À. KEMPIS.

I (GOD) am the ground of thy beseeching,
First, it is My will thou have it,
And then I make thee to will it,
And then I make thee to beseech it ;
And if thou beseech it,
How should it then be that thou
should not have thy beseeching?

Lady Julian of Norwich, fifteenth century.

THE prayers I make will then be sweet indeed,
If Thou the spirit give by which I pray :
My unassisted heart is barren clay,
That of its native self can nothing feed.

Michael Angelo, 1475–1564.

Prayer is a powerful thing, for God has bound and tied Himself thereto.—LUTHER.

PRAYER is the soul's sincere desire,
　　Uttered or unexpressed;
The motion of a hidden fire
　　That trembles in the breast.

Prayer is the burden of a sigh,
　　The falling of a tear,
The upward glancing of an eye
　　When none but God is near.

Prayer is the simplest form of speech
　　That infant lips can try;
Prayer the sublimest strains that reach
　　The Majesty on high.

Prayer is the contrite sinner's voice,
　　Returning from his ways,
While Angels in their songs rejoice,
　　And cry, " Behold, he prays ! "

Prayer is the Christian's vital breath,
　　The Christian's native air,
His watchword at the gates of death:
　　He enters heaven with prayer.

The saints in prayer appear as one
　　In word, and deed, and mind,
While with the Father and the Son
　　Sweet fellowship they find.

O Thou by whom we come to God,
　　The Life, the Truth, the Way,
The path of prayer Thyself hast trod:
　　Lord, teach us how to pray.

　　　　　　　　J. Montgomery, 1771–1854.

No man doth well but God hath part in him.—SWIN-
BURNE.

GOD be in my head,

And in my understanding;

God be in my eyes,

And in my looking;

God be in my mouth,

And in my speaking;

God be in my heart,

And in my thinking;

God be at my end,

And at my departing.

Old Sarum Primer, 1558.

A man's reach should exceed his grasp, Or what's heaven for?—BROWNING.

GIVE me an heart that beats
In all its pulses with the common heart
Of human kind, which the same things make glad,
The same make sorry! Give me grace enough
Even in their first beginnings to detect
The endeavours which the proud heart still is making
To cut itself from off the common root,
To set itself upon a private base,
To have wherein to glory of its own,
Beside the common glory of the kind!
Each such attempt in all its hateful pride
And meanness, give me to detect and loathe,—
A man, and claiming fellowship with men!

Archbishop Trench, 1807–1886.

Shutting out Fear with all the strength of Hope.—
BROWNING.

O GOD our Father, who dost exhort us to pray, and who
dost grant what we ask, if only, when we ask, we live a
better life ; hear me, who am trembling in this darkness,
and stretch forth Thy hand unto me ; hold forth Thy light
before me ; recall me from my wanderings ; and, Thou
being my Guide, may I be restored to myself and to
Thee.

St. Augustine, 354–430.

Prayer is a shield to the soul, a sacrifice to God, and a scourge to Satan.—BUNYAN.

HYMN TO GOD THE FATHER

WILT Thou forgive that sin where I begun,
    Which was my sin, though it were done before?
Wilt Thou forgive that sin, through which I run,
    And do run still : though still I do deplore?
       When Thou hast done, Thou hast not done,
         For I have more.

Wilt Thou forgive that sin by which I have won
    Others to sin, and made my sin their door?
Wilt Thou forgive that sin which I did shun
    A year, or two ; but wallowed in, a score?
       When Thou hast done, Thou hast not done,
         For I have more.

I have a sin of fear, that when I've spun
    My last thread, I shall perish on the shore ;
Swear by Thyself that at my death Thy Son
    Shall shine—as He shines now, and heretofore ;
       And, having done that, Thou hast done,
         I fear no more.

John Donne, 1572–1631.

CANTICLE OF THE SUN

O MOST high, almighty, good Lord God, to Thee belong praise, glory, honour, and all blessing!

Praised be my Lord God with all His creatures, and specially our brother the sun, who brings us the day and who brings us the light; fair is he and shines with a very great splendour; O Lord, he signifies to us Thee!

Praised be my Lord for our sister the moon, and for the stars, the which He has set clear and lovely in heaven.

Praised be my Lord for our brother the wind, and for the air and cloud, calms and all weather by the which Thou upholdest life in all creatures.

Praised be my Lord for our sister water, who is very serviceable unto us and humble and precious and clean.

Praised be my Lord for our brother fire, through whom Thou givest us light in the darkness; and he is bright and pleasant and very mighty and strong.

Praised be my Lord for our mother the earth, the which doth sustain us and keep us, and bringeth forth divers fruits and flowers of many colours, and grass.

Praised be my Lord for all those who pardon one another for His love's sake, and who endure weakness and tribulation; blessed are they who peaceably shall endure, for Thou, O most Highest, shalt give them a crown.

Praised be my Lord for our sister, the death of the body, from which no man escapeth. Woe to him who dieth in mortal sin! Blessed are they who are found walking by Thy most holy will, for the second death shall have no power to do them harm.

Praise ye and bless the Lord, and give thanks unto Him and serve Him with great humility.

St. Francis of Assisi, 1182–1226.

The words that make a man feel strong in speaking Truth.
—TENNYSON.

FROM " THE LITANY "

HEAR us, O hear us, Lord ; to Thee
A sinner is more music, when he prays,

Than spheres' or angels' praises be,
In panegyric allelujahs ;

Hear us, for till Thou hear us, Lord,

We know not what to say ;
Thine ear to our sighs, tears, thoughts, gives voice and word ;
O Thou who Satan heard'st in Job's sick day,
Hear Thyself now, for Thou in us dost pray.

John Donne, 1572–1631.

Learn that the flame of Everlasting Love doth burn ere it transform.—CARDINAL NEWMAN.

TO GOD

Come to me, God; but do not come
To me, as to the gen'ral doom,
In power; or come Thou in that state,
When Thou Thy laws didst promulgate,
Whenas the mountains quak'd for dread,
And sullen clouds bound up his head.
No, lay Thy stately terrors by,
To talk with me familiarly;
For if Thy thunder-claps I hear,
I shall less swoon than die for fear.
Speak Thou of Love, and I'll reply
By way of Epithalamy,
Or sing of mercy, and I'll suit
To it my viol and my lute:
Thus let Thy lips but love distil,
Then come, my God, and hap what will.

Robert Herrick, 1591–1674.

Sublimity always is simple.—LONGFELLOW.

NO COMING TO GOD WITHOUT CHRIST

GOOD and great God! how should I fear
To come to Thee, if Christ not there!
Could I but think He would not be
Present, to plead my cause for me;
To hell I'd rather run, than I
Would see Thy face, and He not by.

Robert Herrick, 1591–1674.

Of all acts, is not for man Repentance the most divine?—
CARLYLE.

TO GOD

GOD, who me gives a will for to repent,
Will add a power, to keep me innocent;
That I shall ne'er that trespass recommit,
When I have done true penance here for it.

Robert Herrick, 1591–1674.

Prayer purifies; it is a self-preached sermon.—JEAN PAUL.

TO GOD

IF I have played the truant, or have here
Fail'd in my part; oh! Thou that art my dear,
My mild, my loving Tutor, Lord and God!
Correct my errors gently with Thy rod.
I know that faults will many here be found,
But where sin dwells, there let Thy grace abound.

Robert Herrick, 1591–1674.

What is man that Thou art mindful of him?—Psalm viii. 4.

PRAYER FOR MEEKNESS

O GOD, whose gracious providence has particularly ordain'd the spirit of meekness to waft us safely through the turbulent sea of the world to our haven of bliss; vouchsafe, we beseech Thee, that the clear experience we every day make of our own weakness and vanity, may so dispose us for this precious virtue that our minds may never be discompos'd with passion, nor our tongues break forth into violent expressions, but our temper may be always preserv'd calm and regular, and, as becometh those, all whose powers are possess'd of the joys of heaven, apt to feel in everything only the sweet impulses of hope and charity, through Our Lord Jesus Christ Thy Son, to whom, with Thee, and the Holy Ghost, be all honour and glory, world without end.

From an Eighteenth-Century Missal.

Thou canst not choose but serve.—ARCHBISHOP TRENCH.

FOR GRACE TO SPEND OUR TIME WELL

O ETERNAL God, who from all eternity dost behold and love Thy own glories and perfections infinite, and hast created me to do the work of God after the manner of men, and to serve Thee in this generation, and according to my capacities ; give me Thy grace, that I may be a curious and prudent spender of my time, so that I may best prevent or resist all temptation, and be profitable to the Christian commonwealth, and by discharging all my duty may glorify Thy Name.

Take from me all slothfulness, and give me a diligent and active spirit, and wisdom to choose my employment, that I may do works proportionate to my person, and to the dignity of a Christian, and may fill up the spaces of my time with actions of religion and charity ; that when the Devil assaults me, he may not find me idle, and my dearest Lord at His sudden coming may find me busy in lawful, necessary, and pious actions, improving my talent intrusted to me by Thee, my Lord ; that I may enter into the joy of my Lord, to partake of His eternal felicities, even for Thy mercy's sake, and for my dearest Saviour's sake.

Dr. Jeremy Taylor, 1613–1667.

Love divine ! all love excelling.—CHARLES WESLEY.

O MY Lord ! If I worship Thee from fear of hell, burn me in hell ; and if I worship Thee from hope of Paradise, exclude me thence ; but if I worship Thee for Thine own sake, then withhold not from me Thine Eternal Beauty.

An Ancient Moslem Prayer.

My life, if Thou preserv'st my life, Thy sacrifice shall be.
—JOSEPH ADDISON.

PROTEGEZ-MOI, mon Seigneur ; mon navire est si petit,
et votre mer est si grande.

French Traditional Prayer.

Peace in believing.—Romans xv. 13.

O LORD our God, teach us, we beseech Thee, to ask Thee aright for the right blessing. Steer Thou the vessel of our life towards Thyself, Thou tranquil Haven of all storm-tossed souls. Show us the course wherein we should go. Renew a willing spirit in us. Let Thy Spirit curb our wayward senses, and guide and enable us into that which is our true good, to keep Thy laws, and in all our works ever-more to rejoice in Thy glorious and gladdening Presence. For Thine is the glory and praise from all Thy saints for ever and ever.

St. Basil, 329–379.

Bears not each human figure the God-like stamp on his fore-head?—LONGFELLOW.

HIS PETITION

IF war, or want shall make me grow so poor,
As for to beg my bread from door to door,
Lord, let me never act that beggar's part,
Who hath Thee in his mouth, not in his heart.
He who asks alms in that so sacred Name,
Without due reverence, plays the cheater's game.

Robert Herrick, 1591–1674.

Words without thoughts never to Heaven go.—HAMLET.

TO GOD

THOU hast promis'd, Lord, to be
With me in my misery;
Suffer me to be so bold
As to speak, Lord, Say and hold.

Robert Herrick, 1591–1674.

Prayer is a study of truth—a sally of the soul into the unfound infinite.—EMERSON.

TO HIS DEAR GOD

I'LL hope no more
For things that will not come :
And, if they do, they prove but cumbersome ;
Wealth brings much woe :
And, since it fortunes so,
'Tis better to be poor,
Than so abound,
As to be drown'd,
Or overwhelm'd with store.

Pale care, avant !
I'll learn to be content
With that small stock Thy bounty gave or lent.
What may conduce
To my most healthful use,
Almighty God, me grant ;
But that, or this,
That hurtful is
Deny Thy suppliant.

Robert Herrick, 1591–1674.

Men ought always to pray and not to faint.—St. Luke
xviii. 1.

> LORD, make me an instrument of Thy peace ;
>
> Where there is hatred, let me sow love ;
>
> Where there is injury, pardon ;
>
> Where there is discord, union ;
>
> Where there is doubt, faith ;
>
> Where there is despair, hope ;
>
> Where there is darkness, light ;
>
> Where there is sadness, joy.

St. Francis of Assisi, 1182–1226.

There is surely a piece of Divinity in us, something that was before the elements, and owes no homage to the sun.—
SIR THOMAS BROWNE.

VIEW ME, LORD, A WORK OF THINE

VIEW me, Lord, a work of Thine :
Shall I then lie drown'd in night ?
Might Thy grace in me but shine,
I should seem made all of light.

But my soul still surfeits so
On the poisoned baits of sin,
That I strange and ugly grow,
All is dark and foul within.

Cleanse me, Lord, that I may kneel
At Thine altar, pure and white :
They that once Thy mercies feel,
Gaze no more on earth's delight.

Worldly joys like shadows fade,
When the heav'nly light appears ;
But the cov'nants Thou hast made,
Endless, know nor days, nor years.

In Thy word, Lord, is my trust,
To Thy mercies fast I fly ;
Though I am but clay and dust,
Yet Thy grace can lift me high.

Thomas Campion, 1567–1620.

Flattery corrupts both the receiver and giver.—EDMUND BURKE.

FOR THE CLEANSING OF THE HEART

STRENGTHEN me, O God, by the grace of Thy Holy Spirit; grant me to be strengthened with might in the inner man, and to put away from my heart all useless anxiety and distress, and let me never be drawn aside by various longings after anything whatever, whether it be worthless or precious; but may I regard all things as passing away, and myself as passing away with them.

For nothing is lasting under the sun, for all things are vanity and vexation of spirit. O, how wise is he who thus regards them.

Grant me, O Lord, heavenly wisdom, that I may learn to seek Thee above all things, and to understand all other things as they are, according to the order of Thy wisdom.

Grant me prudently to avoid the one who flatters me, and patiently to bear with the one who contradicts me; for it is a mark of great wisdom not to be moved by every wind of words, nor to give ear to the wicked flattery of the siren; for thus we shall go on securely in the course we have begun.

Thomas à Kempis, 1380–1471.

In quietness and confidence shall be your strength.—Isaiah
XXX. 15.

O GOD of mountains, stars, and boundless spaces !
O God of Freedom and of joyous hearts !
When Thy Face looketh forth from all men's faces,
There will be room enough in crowded marts :
Brood Thou around me, and the noise is o'er ;
Thy universe my closet with shut door.

Dr. George Macdonald, 1824–1905.

It is godlike for mortal to assist mortal.—PLINY THE ELDER.

IF there be some weaker one,
Give me strength to help him on;
If a blinder soul there be,
Let me guide him nearer Thee;
Make my mortal dreams come true
With the work I fain would do;
Clothe with life the weak intent,
Let me be the thing I meant;
Let me find in Thy employ
Peace that dearer is than joy;
Out of self to love be led,
And to heaven acclimated,
Until all things sweet and good
Seem my natural habitude.

John Greenleaf Whittier, 1807–1892.

Prayer is the slender nerve that moves the muscles of Omnipotence.—MARTIN TUPPER.

OH blessed Lord! How much I need
Thy Light to guide me on my way!
So many hands, that, without heed,
Still touch Thy wounds and make them bleed,
So many feet that day by day
Still wander from Thy fold astray!
Feeble at best is my endeavour!
I see but cannot reach the height
That lies for ever in the Light;
And yet for ever and for ever,
When seeming just within my grasp,
I feel my feeble hands unclasp,
And sink discouraged into night;—
For Thine own purpose Thou has sent
The strife and the discouragement.

Henry Longfellow, 1807–1882.

There must be some great truth underlying the instinct for worship.—SIR OLIVER LODGE.

O LORD, and Master of us all,
    Whate'er our name or sign,
We own Thy sway, we hear Thy call,
    We test our lives by Thine.

Thou judgest us ; Thy purity
    Doth all our lusts condemn ;
The love that draws us nearer Thee
    Is hot with wrath to them ;

Our thoughts lie open to Thy sight ;
    And naked to Thy glance
Our secret sins are in the light
    Of Thy pure countenance.

Yet weak and blinded though we be
    Thou dost our service own ;
We bring our varying gifts to Thee,
    And Thou rejectest none.

To Thee our full humanity,
    Its joys and pains belong ;
The wrong of man to man on Thee
    Inflicts a deeper wrong.

Who hates, hates Thee ; who loves, becomes
    Therein to Thee allied :
All sweet accords of hearts and homes
    In Thee are multiplied.

Apart from Thee all gain is loss,
    All labour vainly done ;
The solemn shadow of Thy Cross
    Is better than the sun.

J. G. Whittier, 1807–1892.

None can be called deformed but the unkind.—" TWELFTH NIGHT."

UNKINDNESS

LORD, make me coy and tender to offend :
In friendship first, I think, if that agree
      Which I intend
    Unto my friend's intent and end.
I would not use a friend as I use Thee.

My friend may spit upon my curious floor :
Would he have gold ? I lend it instantly ;
      But let the poor
    And Thou within them starve at door.
I cannot use a friend as I use Thee.

When that my friend pretendeth to a place,
I quit my interest, and leave it free ;
      But when Thy grace
    Sues for my heart, I Thee displace :
Nor would I use a friend as I use Thee.

Yet can a friend what Thou hast done fulfil ?
O write in brass : " My God upon a tree
      His blood did spill,
    Only to purchase my goodwill " :
Yet use I not my foes as I use Thee.

George Herbert, 1593–1633.

Thy desire, which tends to know the works of God, thereby to glorify the great Work-Master.—MILTON.

DEO. OPT. MAX.

FATHER of All : in every Age,
    In every Clime ador'd,
By Saint, by Savage, and by Sage,
    Jehovah, Jove, or Lord !

Thou Great First Cause, least understood !
    Who all my Sense confin'd
To know but this—that Thou art Good,
    And that myself am blind.

Yet gave me, in this dark Estate,
    To see the Good from Ill ;
And binding Nature fast in Fate,
    Let Conscience free, and Will.

What Conscience dictates to be done,
    Or warns me not to doe,
This, teach me more than Hell to shun,
    That, more than Heav'n pursue.

What Blessings Thy free Bounty gives,
    Let me not cast away ;
For God is pay'd when Man receives ;
    T'enjoy is to obey.

Yet not to Earth's contracted Span
    Thy Goodness led me bound,
Or think Thee Lord alone of Man,
    When thousand Worlds are round.

Let not this weak, unknowing hand
    Presume Thy Bolts to throw,
And deal Damnation round the land,
    On each I judge Thy Foe.

If I am right, Thy Grace impart
    Still in the right to stay :
If I am wrong, oh teach my heart
    To find that Better way.

Save me alike from foolish Pride,
    Or impious Discontent,
At aught Thy Wisdom has deny'd,
    Or aught Thy Goodness lent.

Teach me to feel another's woe ;
    To hide the Fault I see ;
That Mercy I to others show,
    That Mercy show to me.

Mean tho' I am, not wholly so,
    Since quicken'd by Thy Breath,
O lead me wheresoe'er I go,
    Thro' this day's life, or Death :

This day, be Bread and Peace my Lot ;
    All else beneath the Sun,
Thou know'st if best bestow'd, or not :
    And let Thy Will be done.

To Thee, whose Temple is all Space,
    Whose Altar, Earth, Sea, Skies ;
One Chorus let all Being raise :
    All Nature's Incense rise !

Alexander Pope, 1688–1744.

43

Entire simplicity of mind, a thing most sacred in the eyes of Heaven.—WORDSWORTH.

O MY deir hert, young Jesus sweit,
Prepare Thy creddil in my spreit,
And I sall rock Thee in my hert
And never mair from Thee depart.

But I shall praise Thee evermoir
With sangis sweit unto Thy gloir ;
The knees of my hert sall I bow,
And sing that richt Balulalow.

Anonymous.

Nature is the art of God.—SIR THOMAS BROWNE.

PRAYER FOR MICHAELMAS

GOOD Saint Michael, if we must
Leave our bodies here to dust,
Grant our souls a heaven where we
Still your Michaelmas may see.
Do not make me quire and sing
With radiant angels in a ring,
Nor idly tread a pearl-paved street
With my new unearthly feet ;
Do not shut me in a heaven
Golden bright from morn to even,
Where no shadows and no showers
Dim the tedious, shining hours.
Grant that there be autumn still,
Smoke-blue dusk, brown crisp and chill,
And let the furrowed plough-land bare
Curve strongly to the windswept air ;
Make the leafy beechwoods burn
Russet, yellow, bronze by turn,
And set the hedgerow and the briar
Thick with berries red as fire.
Let me search and gather up
Acorns green, with knobbed cup,
And prickly chestnuts, plumping down
To show a glossy kernel brown.
Splendid cities like me ill,
And for song I have no skill ;
Then let me, in an autumn wood,
Sweep, and pick up sticks for God.

Viola Garvin.

A child may say Amen to a bishop's prayer, and feel the way it goes.—ELIZABETH BARRETT BROWNING.

FOR OUR CHILDREN

BLESS my children with healthful bodies, with good understandings, with the graces and gifts of Thy spirit, with sweet dispositions and holy habits, and sanctify them throughout in their bodies and souls and spirits, and keep them inblamable to the coming of the Lord Jesus.

Dr. Jeremy Taylor, 1613–1667.

A profound contemplation of the First Composer.—SIR THOMAS BROWNE.

LORD, make my heart a place where angels sing !
    For surely thoughts low-breathed by Thee
Are angels gliding near on noiseless wing ;
    And where a home they see
Swept clean, and garnish'd with adoring joy,
    They enter in and dwell, and teach that heart to swell
With heavenly Melody, their own untired employ.

John Keble, 1792–1866.

While life is good to give, I give.—SIR EDWIN ARNOLD.

TAKE my life, and let it be
Consecrated, Lord, to Thee ;
Take my moments and my days,
Let them flow in ceaseless praise.
Take my hands, and let them move
At the impulse of Thy love.
Take my feet, and let them be
Swift and beautiful for Thee.

Take my voice, and let me sing
Always, only, for my King ;
Take my lips, and let them be
Filled with messages from Thee.
Take my silver and my gold ;
Not a mite would I withhold.
Take my intellect, and use
Every power as Thou shalt choose.

Take my will, and make it Thine :
It shall be no longer mine.
Take my heart : it is Thine own :
It shall be Thy royal throne.
Take my love ; my Lord, I pour
At Thy feet its treasure-store.
Take myself, and I will be
Ever, only, all for Thee.

Frances R. Havergal, 1836–1879.

He was the Word, that spake it.—JOHN DONNE.

THREE things are of the Evil One:
> An evil eye;
> An evil tongue;
> An evil mind.

Three things are of God, and these three are what Mary told to her Son, for she heard them in Heaven:
> The merciful word,
> The singing word,
> And the good word.

May the power of these three holy things be on all men and women of Erin for evermore, Amen.

Traditional Irish prayer.

If there be any good in thee, believe that there is much more in others—that so thou mayest preserve humility within thee.
—THOMAS À KEMPIS.

O GOD of earth and altar,
    Bow down and hear our cry,
Our earthly rulers falter,
    Our people drift and die ;
The walls of gold entomb us,
    The swords of scorn divide,
Take not Thy thunder from us,
    But take away our pride.

From all that terror teaches,
    From lies of tongue and pen,
From all the easy speeches,
    That comfort cruel men,
From sale and profanation
    Of honour and the sword,
From sleep and from damnation,
    Deliver us, good Lord !

Tie in a living tether
    The prince and priest and thrall,
Bind all our lives together,
    Smite us and save us all ;
In ire and exultation
    Aflame with faith, and free,
Lift up a living nation,
    A single sword to Thee.

G. K. Chesterton, 1874–1936.

DEAR Lord and Father of mankind,
    Forgive our foolish ways !
Re-clothe us in our rightful mind,
In purer lives Thy service find,
    In deeper reverence praise.

In simple trust like theirs who heard,
    Beside the Syrian sea,
The gracious calling of the Lord,
Let us, like them, without a word
    Rise up and follow Thee.

O Sabbath rest by Galilee !
    O calm of hills above,
Where Jesus knelt to share with Thee
The silence of eternity,
    Interpreted by love.

Drop Thy still dews of quietness,
    Till all our strivings cease :
Take from our souls the strain and stress,
And let our ordered lives confess
    The beauty of Thy peace.

Breathe through the heats of our desire
    Thy coolness and Thy balm ;
Let sense be dumb, let flesh retire ;
Speak through the earthquake, wind, and fire,
    O still small voice of calm !

J. G. Whittier, 1807–1892.

The principal part of faith is patience.—GEORGE
MACDONALD.

TAKE from us, O God, all tediousness of spirit, all
impatience and unquietness. Let us possess ourselves in
patience . . . through Jesus Christ our Lord.

Jeremy Taylor, 1613–1667.

Thank God, guilt was never a rational thing.—EDMUND BURKE.

ALMIGHTY God, by whom alone kings reign and princes decree justice, and from whom alone cometh all counsel, wisdom, and understanding,

We, Thine unworthy servants, here gathered together in Thy name, do most humbly beseech Thee to send down the heavenly wisdom from above, to direct and guide us in all our consultations :

And grant that, we having Thy fear always before our eyes, and laying aside all private interests, prejudices, and partial affections, the result of all our counsels may be the glory of Thy blessed name, the maintenance of true religion and justice, and the safety, honour, and happiness of the King, the public welfare, peace and tranquillity of the realm, and the uniting and knitting together of the hearts of all persons and estates within the same in true Christian love and charity towards one another, Through Jesus Christ our Lord and Saviour.

The Prayer of the House of Commons.

[Used at every sitting of the House, and composed by Sir Christopher Yelverton, M.P. for Northampton and Speaker of the House, some time about 1578.]

PAMELA'S PRAYER

O ALL-SEEING Light, and eternal Life of all things, to whom nothing is either so great that it may resist, or so small that it is contemned ; look upon my misery with Thine eye of mercy, and let Thine infinite power vouchsafe to limit out some proportion of deliverance unto me, as to Thee shall seem most convenient. Let not injury, O Lord, triumph over me, and let my faults by Thy hand be corrected, and make not mine enemy the minister of Thy justice. But yet, O Lord, if, in Thy wisdom, this be the aptest chastisement for my inexcusable folly ; if this low bondage be fittest for my over-high desires ; and the pride of my not enough humble heart be thus to be broken, O Lord, I yield unto Thy will, and joyfully embrace what sorrow Thou wilt have me suffer. Only thus much let me crave of Thee—let my craving, O Lord, be accepted of Thee, since even that proceeds from Thee— let me crave (even by the noblest title which in my great affliction I may give myself, that I am Thy creature ; and by Thy goodness, which is Thyself) that Thou wilt suffer some beams of Thy majesty to shine into my mind, that it may still depend confidently on Thee. Let calamity be the exercise, but not the overthrow of my virtue : let their power prevail, but prevail not to destruction. Let my greatness be their prey ; let my pain be the sweetness of their revenge ; let them (if so seem good unto Thee) vex me with more and more punishment. But, O Lord, let never their wickedness have such a hand, but that I may carry a pure mind in a pure body.

Sir Philip Sidney, 1554–1586.

[Copied by Charles the First for his own use.]

By all means use sometimes to be alone!
Salute thyself! See what thy soul doth wear!
—GEORGE HERBERT.

I THANK Thee, Lord, for knowing me better than I know myself, and for letting me know myself better than others know me.

Make me, I pray Thee, better than they suppose, and forgive me what they do not know.

Attributed to Abu Bekr, 572(?)–634, father-in-law of Moham-med and first calif of Islam.

(It is said that he recited it when he heard his people praising him.)

I form'd them free, and free they must remain till they enthrall themselves.—MILTON.

O LET Thine enemies know that Thou hast received England . . . into Thine own protection. Set a wall about it, O Lord, and ever more mightily defend it. Let it be a comfort to the afflicted, a help to the oppressed, and a defence to Thy church and people persecuted abroad. . . . Direct and go before our armies both by sea and land. Bless them and prosper them, and grant unto them Thy honourable success and victory.

Queen Elizabeth, 1558–1603.

[Written when news came that the Armada had sailed. It was read twice a week in all the churches till peace came.]

Great souls are always loyally submissive, reverent to what is over them.—CARLYLE.

O LORD God everlasting, Which reignest over the kingdoms of men . . . so teach me, I humbly beseech Thee, Thy word, and so strengthen me with Thy grace that I may feed Thy people with a faithful and a true heart, and rule them prudently with power. O Lord, Thou hast set me on high. My flesh is frail and weak. If I therefore at any time forget Thee, touch my heart, O Lord, that I may again remember Thee. If I swell against Thee, pluck me down in my own conceit. . . . I acknowledge, O my King, without Thee my throne is unstable, my seat unsure, my kingdom tottering, my life uncertain. I see all things in this life subject to mutability, nothing to continue still at one stay. . . . Create therefore in me, O Lord, a new heart, and so renew my spirit that Thy law may be my study, Thy truth my delight, Thy church my care, Thy people my crown, Thy righteousness my pleasure, Thy service my government; so shall this my kingdom through Thee be established with peace.

Queen Elizabeth, 1558–1603.

[Found after her death in a little book in which she set down her thoughts about God, who, she believed, guided her.]

What's midnight doubt before the dayspring's Faith?—
BROWNING.

O MERCIFUL God, be Thou unto me a strong tower of
defence, I humbly entreat Thee. Give me grace to await
Thy leisure, and patiently to bear what Thou doest unto me;
nothing doubting or mistrusting Thy goodness towards me,
for Thou knowest what is good for me better than I do.
Therefore do with me in all things what Thou wilt; only
arm me, I beseech Thee, with Thine armour, that I may
stand fast; above all things, taking to me the shield of
faith; praying always that I may refer myself wholly to Thy
will, abiding Thy pleasure, and comforting myself in those
troubles which it shall please Thee to send me, seeing such
troubles are profitable for me; and I am assuredly per-
suaded that all Thou doest cannot but be well; and unto
Thee be all honour and glory.

Lady Jane Grey, 1537–1554.

The nobility of labour—the long pedigree of toil.—LONG-
FELLOW.

O LORD God, when Thou givest to Thy servants to
endeavour any great matter, grant us also to know that it is
not the beginning but the continuing of the same until it be
thoroughly finished which yieldeth the true glory.

Sir Francis Drake, 1540–1596.

Every man's task is his life-preserver.—EMERSON.

O LORD, Thou knowest how busy I must be this day. If I forget Thee, do not Thou forget me. . . . March on, boys!

Sir Jacob Astley, on his knees before the Battle of Edgehill,
1642.

*Though I walk through the valley of the shadow of death,
I will fear no evil.*—Psalm xxiii.

LOOK, God, I have never spoken to You,
And now I want to say " How do you do? "
You see, God, they told me You did not exist,
And I, like a fool, believed all this.
Last night, from a shell-hole, I saw Your sky,
I figured that they had told me a lie.
Had I taken time before to see things You had made,
I'd sure have known they weren't calling a spade a spade.

I wonder, God, if You would shake my poor hand?
Somehow I feel You would understand.
Strange I had to come to this hellish place
Before I had time to see Your Face.
Well, I guess, there isn't much more to say,
But I'm glad, God, that I met You to-day.
The zero hour will soon be here,
But I'm not afraid to know that You're near.

The signal has come—I shall soon have to go,
I like You lots—this I want You to know.
I am sure this will be a horrible fight;
Who knows? I may come to Your House to-night.
Though I wasn't friendly to You before,
I wonder, God, if You'd wait at Your door?
Look, I'm shedding tears—*me* shedding tears!
Oh! I wish I'd known You these long, long years.
Well, I have to go now, dear God. Good-bye,
But now that I've met You I'm not scared to die.

*Lines discovered on the dead body of an American soldier killed in
action in North Africa,* 1944.

[They were found by an R.A.M.C. corporal, and printed in a Tunis news-
paper, whence they came to Britain via the United States of America. A friend
of the writer, who was with him when they were written (and who survived the
battle in which the writer was killed), said the soldier was a wild character, but
there were tears running down his face as he wrote the lines.]

Blessed are the valiant that have lived in the Lord.—
CARLYLE.

PRAYER FOR A SOLDIER

ARM me, O Thou God of battles, with courage this day,
that I may not fall before my enemies. The quarrel is
Thine, let the victory be Thine. Tie to my sinews the
strength of David, that I may with a pebble stone strike to
the earth these giants that fight against Thy truth.

So let me fight that, whether I come off lame or sound,
dead or alive, I may live or die Thy soldier.

Thomas Dekker, 1570(?)–1632.

Light is the shadow of God.—17TH-CENTURY SUNDIAL INSCRIPTION.

PER PACEM AD LUCEM

I DO not ask, O Lord, that life may be
   A pleasant road ;
I do not ask that Thou wouldst take from me
   Aught of its load ;

I do not ask that flowers should always spring
   Beneath my feet ;
I know too well the poison and the sting
   Of things too sweet.

For one thing only, Lord, dear Lord, I plead,
   Lead me aright—
Though strength should falter, and though heart
   should bleed—
   Through Peace to Light.

I do not ask, O Lord, that Thou shouldst shed
   Full radiance here ;
Give but a ray of peace, that I may tread
   Without a fear.

I do not ask my cross to understand,
   My way to see—
Better in darkness just to feel Thy hand
   And follow Thee.

Joy is like restless day ; but peace divine
   Like quiet night :
Lead me, O Lord—till perfect Day shall shine,
   Through Peace to Light.

Adelaide Anne Procter, 1825–1864.

They please Him best who labour most to do in peace His Will.—WORDSWORTH.

EVENING

O LORD, who hast given us Thy summer sun to gladden us with his light and to ripen the fruits of the earth for our support, and who biddest him to set when his work is done, that he may rise again to-morrow ; give Thy blessing to us Thy servants, that the lesson of the works of Thy hand may be learnt by us Thy living works, and that we may run our course like the sun which is now gone from us.

Let us rise early and go late to rest, being ever busy and zealous in doing Thy will. Let our light shine before men, that they may glorify Thee, our Heavenly Father. Let us do good all our days, and be useful to and comfort others. And let us finish our course in faith, that we too may rise again to a course which shall never end.

Dr. Thomas Arnold, 1795–1842.

Now may the good God pardon all good men !—ELIZABETH
BARRETT BROWNING.

O LORD, be gracious unto us ! In all that we hear or see, in all that we say or do, be gracious unto us. I ask pardon of the Great God. I ask pardon at the sunset, when every sinner turns to Him. Now and for ever I ask pardon of God. O Lord, cover us from our sins, guard our children and protect our weaker friends.

Bedouin Camel-Drivers' prayer at sunset.

And with a quiet mind go take thy rest.—THOMAS CREECH.

O LORD, support us all the day long of this troublous life, until the shadows lengthen and the evening comes, and the busy world is hushed, and the fever of life is over and our work is done. Then, Lord, in Thy mercy, grant us a safe lodging, a holy rest, and peace at the last.

Used by Cardinal Newman, 1801–1890, but generally thought to be a sixteenth-century prayer.

When He giveth quietness, who then can make trouble?—
Job xxxiv. 29.

O LORD, my God, do Thou Thy holy will!
I will lie still!
I will not stir lest I forsake Thine arm,
And break the charm,
Which lulls me, clinging to my Father's breast
In perfect rest!

John Keble, 1792–1866.

I charge thee, fling away ambition.
By that sin fell the angels : how can man, then,
The image of his Master, hope to win by it?

" HENRY VIII."

How know I, if Thou should'st me raise,
    That I should then raise Thee?
Perhaps great places and Thy praise
    Do not so well agree.

George Herbert, 1583–1648.

JESUS ! Who deemdst it not unmeet
To wash Thine own disciples' feet,
    Though Thou wert Lord of All ;
Teach me thereby this wisdom meek,
That they who self-abasement seek
    Alone shall fear no fall.

F. W. Faber, 1814–1863.

He is rich enough who does not want bread.—ST. JEROME.

TO GOD

GOD! to my little meal and oil
Add but a bit of flesh, to boil:
And Thou my pipkinnet shalt see
Give a wave-offering unto Thee.

Robert Herrick, 1591–1674.

Think, and thank God.—PROVERB.

No ordinary meal—a sacrament awaits us
On our tables daily spread,
For men are risking lives on sea and land
That we may dwell in safety and be fed.

A Grace, told to me in Scotland many years ago.

The angels laugh, too, at the good he has done.—OLIVER
WENDELL HOLMES.

GIVE me a good digestion, Lord,
    And also something to digest;
But when and how that something comes
    I leave to Thee, who knowest best.

Give me a healthy body, Lord;
    Give me the sense to keep it so;
Also a heart that is not bored
    Whatever work I have to do.

Give me a healthy mind, Good Lord,
    That finds the good that dodges sight;
And, seeing sin, is not appalled,
    But seeks a way to put it right.

Give me a point of view, Good Lord,
    Let me know what it is, and why.
Don't let me worry overmuch
    About the thing that's known as " I ".

Give me a sense of humour, Lord,
    Give me the power to see a joke,
To get some happiness from life,
    And pass it on to other folk.

Refectory Grace, Chester Cathedral.

[Written by Thomas Harry Basil Webb (only son of the
late Lt.-Col. Sir Henry Webb, of Caerleon, Mon.) when a
boy at Winchester. As a subaltern in the Welsh Guards,
he was killed in the First World War.]

Revealing by felicity, foretelling by simplicity.—HARTLEY COLERIDGE.

GRACE FOR A CHILD

HERE, a little child, I stand,
Heaving up my either hand:
Cold as paddocks * though they be,
Here I lift them up to Thee,
For a benison to fall
On our meat and on our all.

Robert Herrick, 1591–1674.

* Frogs or toads.

The cause of freedom is the cause of God.—WILLIAM LISLE
BOWLES.

GRACE

FOR good fellowship in freedom and for those who made
it possible, we give thanks.

*(I have been asked by friends to include this grace, which I wrote
and used as chairman of the Paternosters Club during the Battle of
Britain.—C. H.)*

Peace let us seek, to steadfast things attune calm expectations.
—WORDSWORTH.

THAT THE GOOD WILL OF GOD MAY BE FULFILLED

GRANT me, O most merciful Jesus, Thy grace, that it may be with me, and labour with me, and abide with me even to the end.

Give me grace ever to desire and to will what is most acceptable to Thee, and most pleasing in Thy sight. Let Thy Will be mine, and let my will ever follow Thine, and fully accord with it.

Let there be between Thee and me but one will, so that I may love what Thou lovest and abhor what Thou hatest ; and let me not be able to will anything which Thou dost not will, nor to dislike anything which Thou dost will.

Grant that I may die to all things which are on the earth, and for Thy sake love to be despised, and to be unknown in the world.

Grant to me, above all things to be desired, that I may rest in Thee, and that my heart may find its peace in Thee. Thou art the peace of my heart, Thou its sole repose ; out of Thee all things are hard and unquiet.

In this very peace, that is in Thyself, the Sole, the Supreme, the Eternal Good, I will sleep and take my rest.

Thomas à Kempis, 1380–1471.

God oft hath a great share in a little house.—PROVERB
SELECTED BY GEORGE HERBERT.

THANKSGIVING TO GOD FOR HIS HOUSE

LORD, Thou hast given me a cell
    Wherein to dwell ;
A little house, whose humble roof
    Is weather-proof ;
Under the spars of which I lie
    Both soft and dry ;
Where Thou my chamber for to ward
    Has set a guard
Of harmless thoughts, to watch and keep
    Me, while I sleep.
Low is my porch, as is my fate,
    Both void of state ;
And yet the threshold of my door
    Is worn by th' poor,
Who thither come and freely get
    Good words, or meat :
Like as my parlour, so my hall
    And kitchen's small :
A little buttery, and therein
    A little bin,
Which keeps my little loaf of bread
    Unchipp'd, unflead :
Some brittle sticks of thorn or briar
    Make me a fire,
Close by whose living coal I sit,
    And glow like it.
Lord, I confess too, when I dine,
    The pulse is Thine,
And all those other bits, that be
    There plac'd by Thee ;

75

The worts, the purslain, and the mess
        Of water-cress,
Which of Thy kindness Thou hast sent ;
        And my content
Makes those and my beloved beet
        To be more sweet.
'Tis Thou that crown'st my glittering hearth
        With guiltless mirth,
And giv'st me wassail bowls to drink,
        Spic'd to the brink.
Lord, 'tis Thy plenty-dropping hand,
        That soils my land ;
And gives me, for my bushel sown,
        Twice ten for one :
Thou mak'st my teeming hen to lay
        Her egg each day :
Besides my healthful ewes to bear
        Me twins each year :
The while the conduits of my kine
        Run cream (for wine).
All these, and better Thou dost send
        Me, to this end,
That I should render, for my part,
        A thankful heart ;
Which, fir'd with incense, I resign
        As wholly Thine ;
But the acceptance, that must be,
        My Christ, by Thee.

                        Robert Herrick, 1591–1674.

In the delight that work alone can give.—LONGFELLOW.

TEACH me, my God and King,
　　In all things Thee to see,
And what I do in anything,
　　To do it as for Thee !
All may of Thee partake,
　　Nothing can be so mean,
Which with this tincture (for Thy sake)
　　Will not grow bright and clean.
A servant with this clause
　　Makes drudgery divine !
Who sweeps a room as for Thy laws
　　Makes that and th'action fine.

George Herbert, 1593–1633.

The enduring power, not ourselves, which makes for righteousness.—MATTHEW ARNOLD.

FROM the ingrained fashion
Of this earthly nature,
That mars Thy creature ;
From grief—that is but passion ;
From mirth—that is but feigning ;
From tears—that bring no healing ;
From wild and weak complaining—
Thine old strength revealing,—save, oh, save !

Matthew Arnold, 1822–1888.

Guided by faith and matchless fortitude.—MILTON.

O LORD, help me to understand that You ain't gwine to let nuthin' come my way that You and me together can't handle.

Repeated by a negro boy who was running a losing race :

LAWD, You pick 'em up, and I'll put 'em down. You pick 'em up, and I'll put 'em down. . . .

Negro Prayers.

A short prayer finds its way to Heaven.—WILLIAM LANGLAND.

EJACULATIONS

LORD, give me this day my daily opinion, and forgive me the one I had yesterday.

O LORD, convert the world—and begin with me. (*A Chinese student's prayer.*)

Pray God, keep us simple! (*Thackeray.*)

O Lord, make my enemies ridiculous. (*Voltaire.*)

O Lord, preserve me from my friends. I can deal with my enemies myself. (*Ferney.*)

Even, O God, if Thou givest me nothing I will thank Thee for everything.

O God, grant that I may be right—for Ye ken I never change! (*Scots.*)

Bernard Baruch tells that when one of his coloured maids heard that he was appointed adviser to the Office of War Mobilisation, she exclaimed fervently: "Jesus, prop him up!"

God send us all good wives, every man to his wish in this kind, and me mine. (*Richard Burton.*)

O Lord, preserve me from becoming a good man. (*Abbé Geronte.*)

Forgive how I have failed, who saw'st me strive.—
LYTTON.

PRAYER FOR GENEROSITY

TEACH us, good Lord, to serve Thee as Thou deservest :

To give and not to count the cost ;

To fight and not to heed the wounds ;

To toil and not to seek for rest ;

To labour and not to ask for any reward

Save that of knowing that we do Thy will.

St. Ignatius Loyola, 1491–1556.

No sound ought to be heard in the church but the healing voice of Christian charity.—BURKE.

O GOD, make the door of this house wide enough to receive all who need human love and fellowship; narrow enough to shut out all envy, pride and strife.

Make its threshold smooth enough to be no stumbling-block to children, nor to straying feet, but rugged and strong enough to turn back the tempter's power. God make the door of this house the gateway to Thine eternal kingdom.

Ruined St. Stephen's Walbrook, London.

Whatsoever ye do, do all to the glory of God.—I Corinthians x. 31.

HIS PRAYER FOR ABSOLUTION

FOR those my unbaptized rhymes,
Writ in my wild unhallowed times;
For every sentence, clause, and word,
That's not inlaid with Thee, (my Lord)
Forgive me, God, and blot each line
Out of my book, that is not Thine.
But if, 'mongst all, Thou find'st here one
Worthy Thy benediction;
That one of all the rest shall be
The glory of my work, and me.

Robert Herrick, 1591–1674.

With the rays of morn on their white shields of expectation.
—J. R. LOWELL.

HIS LITANY TO THE HOLY SPIRIT

In the hour of my distress,
When temptations me oppress,
And when I my sins confess,
  Sweet Spirit, comfort me!

When I lie within my bed,
Sick in heart and sick in head,
And with doubts discomforted,
  Sweet Spirit, comfort me!

When the house doth sigh and weep,
And the world is drown'd in sleep,
Yet mine eyes the watch do keep,
  Sweet Spirit, comfort me!

When the artless doctor sees
No one hope, but of his fees,
And his skill runs on the lees,
  Sweet Spirit, comfort me!

When his potion and his pill
Has, or none, or little skill,
Meet for nothing but to kill,
  Sweet Spirit, comfort me!

When the passing-bell doth toll,
And the furies in a shoal
Come to fright a passing soul,
  Sweet Spirit, comfort me!

When the tapers now burn blue,
And the comforters are few,
And that number more than true,
  Sweet Spirit, comfort ne!

When the priest his last hath pray'd,
And I nod to what is said,
'Cause my speech is now decay'd;
  Sweet Spirit, comfort me!

    Robert Herrick, 1591–1674.

There is nothing the body suffers that the soul may not profit by.—MEREDITH.

FOR USE IN SICK ROOMS

O LORD and heavenly Father, we come before Thee with our humble thanks for all Thy mercies towards us, more especially for the means of grace which Thou hast afforded us in this interruption to our usual course of health. We thank Thee for thus reminding us that our enjoyment of the blessings of this world will not last for ever—that the things in which we commonly take delight will one day cease to please us. We thank Thee that by calling us off for a little while from our common employments and amusements, Thou givest us time to think how we are passing our life, and what those joys are which if we once learn to know them will abide with us for ever.

Lord, deliver us from all impatience and from all fear of our bodies, and fill us at the same time with spiritual fear ; let us not be afraid of pain or sickness, but let us be afraid of Thee and not waste the opportunity which Thou art now affording us.

Give us grace to think under the visitations of light sickness whether we are fit to be visited with dangerous sickness ; let us consider what we should be if, while our body were weakened, our mind should be clouded also, so that we could not then pray to Thee for succour.

Now, therefore, O Lord, teach us to call on Thee while we can call on Thee, to think on Thee while our reason is yet in its vigour. Teach us to look into our heart and life, to consider how Thou wouldest judge us, to ask Thy forgiveness through Thy Son Jesus Christ, for all that Thou seest amiss in us, and by the help of Thy Holy Spirit to overcome all that is evil in our heart, and to learn and practise all that is good.

Restore us in Thy good time to our usual health, and grant that this interruption to it may be sanctified to our soul's health, so making it not an evil to us, but an infinite blessing.

Dr. Thomas Arnold, 1795–1842.

My strength is made perfect in weakness.—II Corinthians
xii. 9.

LORD, teach me the art of patience whilst I am well,
and give me the use of it when I am sick. In that day
either lighten my burden or strengthen my back. Make
me, who so often in my health have discovered my weakness
presuming on my own strength, to be strong in my sickness
when I solely rely on Thy assistance.

Thomas Fuller, 1608–1661.

Of all acts, is not for man repentance the most divine?—
CARLYLE.

A PRAYER, IN PROSPECT OF DEATH

O THOU unknown, Almighty Cause
    Of all my hope and fear !
In whose dread Presence, ere an hour,
    Perhaps I must appear !

If I have wander'd in those paths
    Of life I ought to shun ;
As something, loudly in my breast,
    Remonstrates I have done ;

Thou know'st that Thou hast formed me
    With passions wild and strong ;
And list'ning to their witching voice
    Has often led me wrong.

Where human weakness has come short,
    Or frailty stept aside,
Do Thou, All-Good, for such Thou art,
    In shades of darkness hide.

Where with intention I have err'd,
    No other plea I have,
But, Thou art good ; and goodness still
    Delighteth to forgive.
                    Robert Burns, 1759–1796.

Mercy first and last shall brightest shine.—MILTON.

HERE lie I, Martin Elginbrodde :
Hae mercy on my soul, Lord God,
As I would do, were I Lord God
And Ye were Martin Elginbrodde.
Elgin Cathedral Epitaph.

There may be worship without words.—LONGFELLOW.

GOD give me work
Till my life shall end
And life
Till my work is done.

*On the grave of Winifred
Holtby, Novelist, 1898–
1935, at Rudston, Yorkshire.*

The still small voice of gratitude.—GRAY.

My prayers and alms, imperfect and defiled,
Were but the feeble efforts of a child ;
Howe'er performed, it was their brightest part,
That they proceeded from a grateful heart.

William Cowper, 1731–1800.

To steadfast things attune calm expectations.—WORDS-
WORTH.

SONG OF SIMEON

LORD, now lettest thou Thy servant depart in peace,
according to Thy word :

For mine eyes have seen Thy salvation. . . .

Luke ii. 28–29.

His mind was a thanksgiving to the Power that made him.
—WORDSWORTH.

ANTIPHON

LET all the world in every corner sing,
   My God and King!
The heavens are not too high,
His praise may thither fly:
The earth is not too low,
His praises there may grow.
Let all the world in every corner sing,
   My God and King!

Let all the world in every corner sing,
   My God and King!
The Church with psalms must shout,
No door can keep them out:
But, above all, the heart
Must bear the longest part.
Let all the world in every corner sing,
   My God and King!

       George Herbert, 1593–1633.

Be ye transformed by the renewing of your mind.—Romans
xii. 2.

FINALLY, brethren, whatsoever things are true, whatsoever things are honest, whatsoever things are just, whatsoever things are pure, whatsoever things are lovely, whatsoever things are of good report; if there be any virtue,
and if there be any praise, think on these things.

Philippians iv. 8–11.

INDEX

INDEX OF FIRST LINES